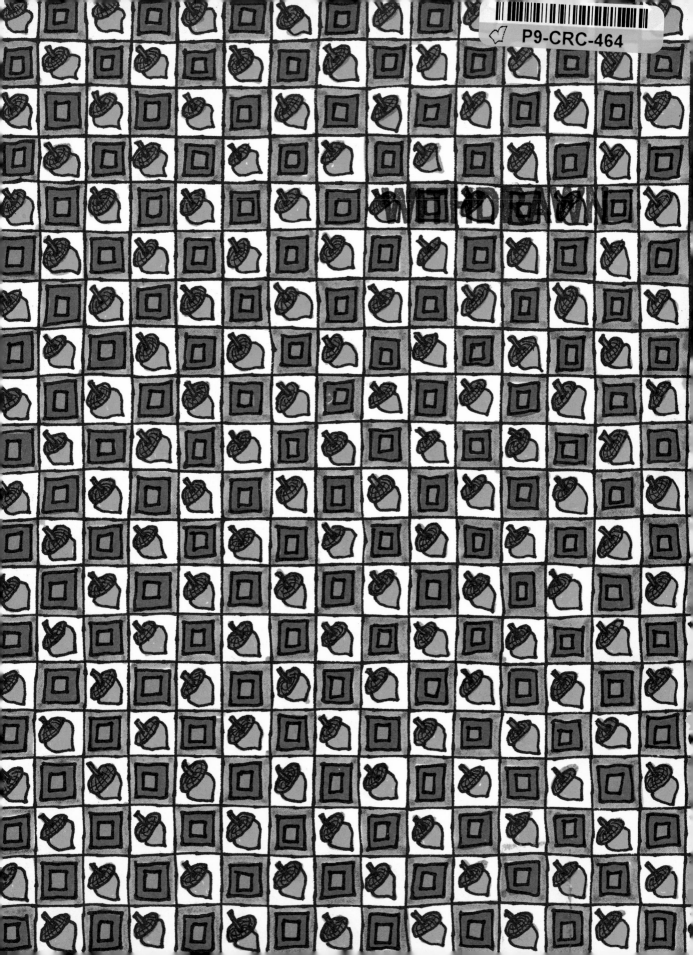

HOW THE RABBIT STOLE THE MOON

LOUISE MOERI

Illustrated by Marc Brown

HOUGHTON MIFFLIN COMPANY BOSTON 1977

FOR NEAL — FOR COURAGE

Also by Louise Moeri
STAR MOTHER'S YOUNGEST CHILD

Library of Congress Cataloging in Publication Data

Moeri, Louise.
 How the rabbit stole the moon.

 SUMMARY: Tells the story of how a rabbit stole
part of the sun and created the moon and stars.
 [1. Moon — Fiction. 2. Animals — Fiction]
I. Brown, Marc Tolon. II. Title.
PZ7.M7214Hq   [E]   77-3158
ISBN 0-395-25765-4

There was a time when the world was altogether dark at night. Throughout the day the Sun flamed and rolled in the sky like a hot, red bird, but at night when he went to roost in the rocky crags of the western rim he took all his light with him and everything was left in cold and darkness. In the terrible gloom the animals huddled in their dens, hungry and fearful.

"Watch for a storm," the fox said. "When the lightning flares you can see at night—for a little while."

"But lightning doesn't last long enough," growled the slow-moving bear. "I need to see at night so I can eat roots and berries and grow fat enough to sleep through the winter."

"Remember how the mountains sometimes turn to fire?" said the beaver. "That makes a *great* light—I can see clear across my pond."

"Yes, but when that happens, the forest burns and many lives are lost," said the raven. "No one wants to see others suffer."

"What can we do about the darkness?" asked the wolf. "No one hates it more than I. I need more time to hunt for food—my cubs are hungry."

Then the great elk spoke. "There is only one course for us to take," he said. "One of us will have to go to the Sun and ask him to give us some of his light to shine through the night. He has so much—he can easily spare some."

It was agreed that this was a good plan. Since the elk had proposed the idea, he himself offered to go and speak with the Sun.

The very next morning he set out. He looked around and found the highest mountain in all the world, and then began to climb it so he could be as near to the Sun as possible. The mountain was so high that he climbed for three days, resting in the terrible darkness every night in whatever glen or cranny he could find.

Late in the afternoon of the third day, the great elk toiled wearily up the last windswept crag until—finally —there he stood, looking square into the face of the Sun, who now was close overhead.

"Generous Sun!" said the elk, "my friends and I have great need of some of your light to help us through the long, dark nights. Pray, I beg you, spare us some — you are so rich in those golden beams!"

But the Sun flamed and rolled and his hot, red rays crackled around him. "Never! Never!" he shouted. "I've none too much for myself!"

So the elk had to go back home, all the way down the highest mountain in the world, walking for three days and at night sleeping wherever he could in glens and crannies. When he got home he told his friends that the Sun would not share his light.

"Let *me* try," growled the bear. "I'll scold and scare the Sun, and *make* him share his light."

So the bear set out, and he too took the path that led to the top of the highest mountain in the world. Since

he had such short legs, it took the bear five whole days, climbing during the daylight hours, and sleeping at night in whatever glens and crannies he could find, until he reached the last windswept crag.

When he got there, he shouted: "Great Sun! Perhaps you have not heard how strong we are on earth! If you don't share some of your light with us to brighten the dark nights, we will declare war on you, and you will shine no more!"

But the Sun flamed and rolled and his hot, red rays
crackled around him. "Never! Never!" he cried. "No
one is more powerful than I! I am the Sun!" And the
whole world shook under his great voice.

So the bear was forced to go all the way back down the highest mountain in the world, walking for five days and sleeping wherever he could at night in glens and crannies. When he got home he told his friends that he had not been able to make the Sun share his light.

"Let *me* go," said the snake. "I am cunning and sly. Maybe I can persuade the Sun to help us."

So the snake set out. But it took him nine whole days to wriggle through the forests and across the rocky places, sleeping at night in whatever glens or crannies he could find, to make his way up the highest mountain in the world.

At last the snake lay coiled on the topmost wind-swept crag, and he called to the Sun overhead: "Noble Sun! Handsome Sun! If you will only give us some of your light to brighten our dark nights, we will honor you with the title of god, and make sacrifices to you, and build temples in your name!"

But the Sun flamed and rolled and his hot, red rays crackled around him. "Never! Never!" he cried. "No sacrifice, no puny temple, would repay me for the loss of part of myself!"

So the snake had to turn back, creeping all the way down the highest mountain in the world, wriggling for nine whole days through the forests and across the rocky places, sleeping at night in whatever glen or cranny he could find.

All the animals were too disheartened to try again. If the great elk, the powerful bear, the cunning snake, had failed, who among them could hope to do better?

Then the rabbit came forward. "Let *me* go," he said. "Perhaps the Sun will not take offense at me. I am small and insignificant—he may even take pity on me."

A great wave of laughter swept over the animal kingdom. That foolish rabbit! A small, weak creature with nothing to recommend him but four big front teeth and four speedy legs—how could *he* ever hope to succeed?

In spite of their jeers, the rabbit set off. The road was steep and rough and the going difficult, and soon he began to see that the journey would take him a long, long time. Days passed as he crept up and down the sides of mountains and hopped fearfully along through dense, somber thickets. Danger threatened many

times and he was forced to waste precious time hiding and creeping. For seventeen days he traveled the road toward the highest mountain in the world, through forests and across rocky places, sleeping at night in whatever glens and crannies he could find.

But at last he reached the topmost windswept crag, and he called to the Sun overhead: "Brother Sun, please give us some of your rays to light our fearful dark nights, for are we not brothers, all?"

But the Sun flamed and rolled and his hot, red rays crackled around him. "Never! Never!" he cried. "*I have no brothers!*"

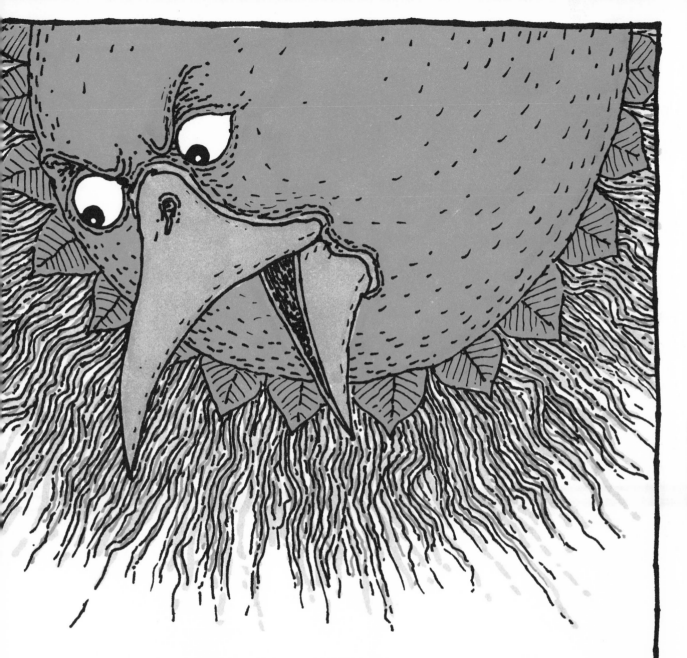

Now, the rabbit knew he was the last animal who
would ever speak to the Sun. Everyone depended on
him. He gathered his powerful hind legs under him and
sprang up—UP—UP—and fastened his big front
teeth on the edge of the Sun! Before the Sun knew what
was happening, the rabbit had bitten a great piece out
of it. And when he fell back to earth, the rabbit started
to run!

He ran like the wind itself—leaping and falling and tumbling, but always racing forward. Holding the huge piece of the Sun between his sharp front teeth, he streaked down the side of the world's highest mountain —through forests—across rocky places. He didn't even stop to sleep. Soon he began to tire, but still he drove himself onward.

At the top of the very last high hill, just as it was get-ting dark, the rabbit stubbed his toe. And there went his piece of the Sun rolling and tumbling down the hill to the very bottom—where it *smashed*!

The rabbit's heart was broken. How could he have been so careless as to get his great bite of the Sun so near home, and then let it fall?

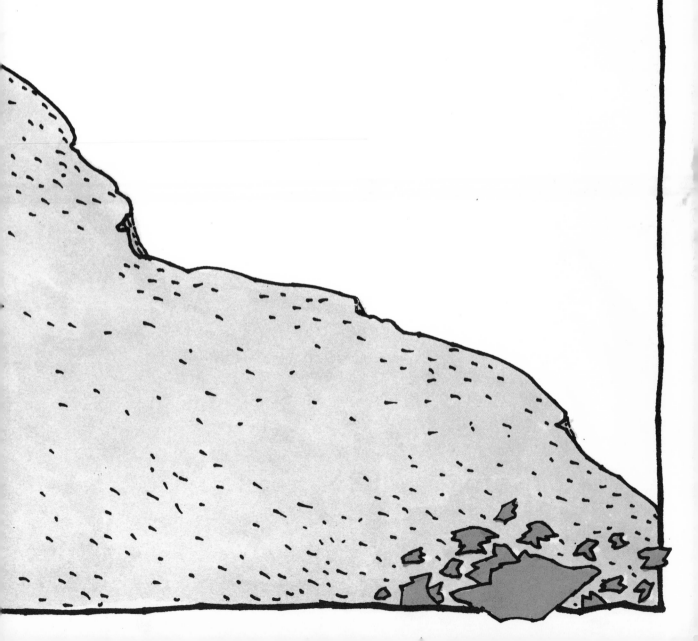

He limped down the hill and looked at the fallen pieces. One was a great deal larger than all the rest and Rabbit picked it up. "Well," he said sadly, "it may not be as big as I had hoped, but even this little light will help us."

And he leaned far back and gave a great heave and threw the biggest chunk of the Sun up into the twilight sky.

There it hung!

A magical radiance spread all over the world. For the very first moment in all of time, a silvery light glanced off every rock, turning it to crystal, and transforming each leaf and blade of grass into a spear of frost. Sparks danced in the ripples of lakes and rivers. All the animals stood silent as they watched the world's first moon spread its glow through the dark sky.

Then the rabbit looked down at the smaller pieces of the Sun that still lay scattered on the grass. His heart ached. "They are so beautiful too!" he cried. "There must be a way to save them!" Then he picked up one of the pieces and threw it into the sky.

There it sparkled, a tiny, glimmering pinpoint of light against the deep blue sky.

"How beautiful!" cried the animals.

So the rabbit quickly threw all the other pieces up—
even the tiniest ones!

And when he had finished, there was the sky shimmering with the loveliest of lights—the moon and stars!

Ever since that time, the moon has always remembered how she was stolen from the Sun. There are times when the moon dreams about the old, old days, and if you look up on certain nights you will see that the moon looks exactly like a great big bite taken from the golden sun.

And the rabbit? Well, he dreams too, and so do all his tribe. To this very day, all rabbits love to go out and run and play—and even dance, I'm told—in the moonlight, in celebration of the old, old time when the rabbit stole the moon!